By the Power Vested in

Y O U

By the Power Vested in

YU

How to Officiate a Wedding

A Guide for Ordained Ministers

Brother G. Martin Freeman

Dedication

To **you,** our ministers.
We are so proud and so grateful
for the good that you do in the universe every day.

Thank you.

A note about this book:

The Universal Life Church advocates proudly and fiercely that all loving individuals should have the ability to get married. External hierarchical structures should not be permitted undue power over a person's spiritual or personal wellbeing/happiness.

Throughout this guide, we will occasionally make reference to the two individuals involved in the wedding ceremony as the "Bride" and "Groom". We do this for convenience' sake, and apologize if it causes any offense.

When the situation demands, we would welcome you to mentally replace "Bride" and/or "Groom" with the more appropriate term.

Contents

Introduction

As a wedding officiant, you have the privilege of overseeing the beautiful moment when two hearts join together. Regardless of the form the ceremony takes, the wedding is often one of the most important days in a couple's life. It is an honor to be asked to be a minister, but also places on you the serious responsibility of facilitating a wonderful experience for everyone involved. The goal of this guide is to help you learn more about what you can do before, during, and after the wedding ceremony to ensure that the wedding day is a pleasant one for the couple and for their guests.

Though there are common trends and traditions for weddings, many couples prefer to have more non-traditional ceremonies. By asking a friend or family member to officiate, a couple can create the wedding ceremony of their dreams. If you are asked to officiate at a wedding, then you should take time to talk with the bride and groom about their preferences, and use the information in this book to help you prepare the wedding according to their wishes.

Online Resources

Online you will find a number of resources that provide direction and guidance for wedding ministers. We would especially like to invite you to visit our website, www.themonastery.org, where you will be able to get ordained, obtain church supplies, and access our complete online library of wedding and ministry-related information.

On our website, you will find examples of wedding scripts, detailed breakdowns of the relevant legal code in particular areas, full how-to guides and videos explaining how to perform a variety of ceremonies, thought-provoking blogs and sermons, comprehensive analyses of various global religions, and more.

This Guide

After being asked to perform a wedding, chances are that many thoughts and feelings are running through your mind. You may be honored, surprised, or excited, but you may also be unsure or nervous. Fear not, for reading this guide will teach you everything you need to know to perform an amazing wedding ceremony.

Think about the all the weddings you've been to during your life. You've probably been a guest many times, in the wedding party a few times, and maybe even one of the betrothed.

As you likely recall, there are a number of different players in a wedding: tens (or hundreds) of guests, perhaps a dozen in the wedding party, and two at the altar... but only one minister. This means that you, as the officiant, have a tremendous responsibility of single-handedly leading everyone present through the personal, powerful ceremony.

Understanding this responsibility will allow you to approach your role with the proper mindset. Though there is great significance and gravity in the part you must play, don't forget that a wedding is not a solemn event, but rather one of love and joy! You have been blessed with the wonderful opportunity to be involved in a union that is simultaneously deeply spiritual and legally significant.

As the officiant guides a proper wedding ceremony, this book will guide you to be a proper officiant. Whether or not this is your first time officiating a wedding, you will find plenty here to help you. This guide will walk you through the preparations you should make before the ceremony, the actions you'll take during the ceremony, and the things you need to keep in mind once the ceremony is over to ensure that all the loose ends are tied off. You'll also be treated to a number of ideas that can be utilized in crafting a truly unique, customized ceremony.

Read through these pages carefully, make notes, and keep in mind that there is only one officiant at the wedding: **you**. The information in this guide will help you remain vigilant in your preparations, but don't forget the couple plays a major role as well. Together you can visualize the perfect ceremony, and *by the power vested in you*, make it reality!

Before the Ceremony

In this section we will examine the things that you need to consider before the ceremony. A great deal of stress can be avoided by completing these things well ahead of the wedding ceremony instead of waiting until the last moment.

Ordination

In the United States, most states recognize pastors, priests, clergymen, officiants, ministers, judges and justices of the peace as people who are authorized to solemnize a marriage. Each state has unique criteria for who can legally officiate; you should verify the rules within your state before performing any weddings.

In most areas of the country, ministers who were ordained online by the Universal Life Church can perform legally-binding weddings. Various organizations provide an opportunity for people to become ordained ministers in order to perform weddings, though the Universal Life Church is easily the largest and most widely-recognized among these. Those who are not affiliated with a specific religious denomination often seek a non-denominational ordination through the Universal Life Church.

Many ministers of the Universal Life Church became ordained because they were asked by a couple they knew personally to officiate their wedding. We frequently hear from ministers who enjoyed performing their first wedding so much that they go on to officiate another, and then another. Many have even found success as professional wedding officiants, building stable careers!

The easiest, surest, and quickest way to complete your legal ordination online is by going through the Universal Life Church (www.themonastery.org/ordination). The advantage of an ordination through the ULC is that the doors are open to anyone interested in becoming ordained, regardless of that individual's specific spiritual or religious beliefs. If you would like to become ordained to perform ceremonies like weddings, baptisms, or funerals, then you can go through the online ordination process to receive your credentials.

In some counties you might be asked to provide documentation showing that you can legally perform a wedding; you can request this documentation from the Universal Life Church. It is a good idea to keep your credentials on hand when you are performing the ceremony in case you need to show proof that you are an ordained minister.

State & County Laws[1]

As the officiant, you need to make sure that the wedding ceremony is held in accordance with state and local laws. Across most of the country a number of officials are legally allowed to perform weddings, including judges and members of the clergy. Ordained ministers of the Universal Life Church have the authority to officiate weddings in every state except Virginia and parts of Pennsylvania.

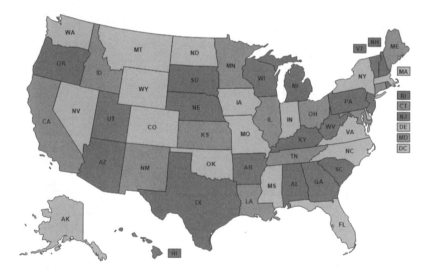

That said, marriage laws are governed at the local level, and you will find that they can vary significantly from one county to the next. After you've gotten ordained, we would urge you to contact the office of your local marriage authority (typically the county clerk) for additional information pertinent to your

1. The Universal Life Church is not a law firm and does not purport to give legal advice regarding any one individual's specific situation. If you have questions or concerns about the legality of a marriage we would advise you to speak to the relevant legal authority and/or confer with a licensed attorney.

specific situation.

On our website we've compiled the Internet's most comprehensive archive of wedding law knowledge pertinent in the United States and beyond (located at http://www.themonastery.org/wedding-laws/). If you haven't already, we invite you to visit this section and navigate to the page created for your specific location. There, you can review detailed information about the steps you must take to get ordained and legally officiate a valid marriage in your area.

Please take the time to review and understand the laws that affect you as a minister. Acting as a wedding officiant is tremendously rewarding, but it is also a serious responsibility. You will want to ensure that you are operating per the requirements of the State so that the weddings you officiate are legally binding. If you are having trouble locating the laws surrounding marriage in your area, the marriage laws section of our website referenced above will, in addition to providing some basic insight, refer you to the relevant legal code. You are also welcome to contact a member of our support staff so that we can point you in the right direction.

Paperwork

Solemnizing a marriage is a serious legal responsibility. As such, you should establish a written contract for each wedding that you are asked/hired to perform. You can use a general contract for each wedding, and fill in the names of the bride and groom, as well as the date, time and location of the ceremony.

If you charge a fee for the wedding ceremony services, we'd recommend that you request a deposit when the contract is signed. These details are best worked out well in advance, so that you don't have to worry about paperwork or payments on the day of the wedding.

Depending on your location, either one or both members of the couple will be required to go to the office of the local marriage authority to pick up a copy of their marriage license. It is very important that both they and you fully comprehend the rules that have been established to govern these documents.

Location

The bride and groom will usually have a location selected for their ceremony, but sometimes they might ask their minister for advice about choosing a venue. Popular locations include churches, country clubs, and reception halls. However, the possibilities are unlimited!

Some couples choose to have their wedding ceremony on the beach, in the mountains, in a backyard, at the park, in a dance club, or even on a boardwalk. Whether the ceremony is being planned to take place on a public or private property, you should verify that the group has permission to perform the ceremony in that location.

As the wedding officiant, it can be beneficial to visit the wedding location in advance, so that you are familiar with the venue and can make ceremony plans accordingly. For example, if the couple has requested a traditional activity, like a candle-lighting ceremony, you can work to position the couple so that they are visible to all of the guests. Similarly, you might use the opportunity to conduct an investigation of any challenging factors the venue might present

(e.g. is there a lot of ambient noise?). A wedding rehearsal provides the perfect opportunity to work through any of the logistical considerations referenced above that ought to be addressed before the ceremony with the wedding party.

If the couple doesn't have a rehearsal planned, you should strongly suggest that they hold one. Wedding ceremonies require a great deal of precision. Given the importance of the wedding ceremony all steps should be taken to ensure that it both flows smoothly and adheres to the couple's wishes. If it is an especially small wedding a formal rehearsal may not be necessary. Any rehearsal that does take place should include as much of the wedding party as possible (bridesmaids, groomsmen, the  flower girl, etc.). It's important that everyone with a role to play has a complete understanding of her or his personal responsibilities and understands where she or he needs to be.

Another advantage of an on-location rehearsal is that it provides an opportunity for the bride and groom to review the entire ceremony and discuss any last minute details, allowing you to put the finishing touches on your plans.

Making it Legal

A bride and groom can plan a party, get dressed up, and walk down the aisle... but without an ordained minister, the wedding won't be legally binding! As an ordained minister of the Universal Life Church acting as a wedding officiant, you are not only responsible for being the "master of ceremonies" for the big event, but must also act as the representative of the ULC in asserting the legal validity of the union before the State.

Most counties require that the minister show some form of documentation proving their affiliation with the Universal Life Church. As mentioned earlier in this guide, the type of documentation required will vary county-to-county, and you should get in touch with the local marriage authority (typically the county clerk's office) to find out exactly what you need. The Universal Life Church makes every form of documentation you may require available in its online catalog, be it an ordination credential, a letter of good standing, and/

or anything more. These documents display to the State (and to the wedding couple) that you have the legal right to perform the marriage ceremony. The bride and groom won't necessarily take the time to check the laws, which is understandable given the fact that they are likely busy planning their wedding! As the minister, part of your job is to ensure the local laws are understood and obeyed.

Additionally, it is important for the bride and groom to contact the local authority that issues the marriage license, so that they have it in hand at the time of the ceremony. Often, marriage licenses are only legally valid for 30 days (though this varies significantly by state), and will need to be obtained by the couple, signed, and returned to the issuing office within that window.

After the wedding is complete, find a moment to pull the bride and groom aside and ask them to sign the marriage license. You (as officiant) will need to sign the license as well. Many states also require signatures from witnesses who attended the ceremony.

Tailoring Your Message

As you are preparing for the wedding, you should make time to sit down with the bride and groom to discuss their personal beliefs. A keen understanding of the couple's beliefs will aid you in creating an especially personalized ceremony.

In the appendix of this guide we have provided a worksheet containing a few questions in hopes of helping you to more carefully craft your language. The more you learn about the couple, the more able you will be to put together a ceremony that adheres closely to their desires. You might also, with the couple, take the guest list into consideration in order to avoid offending anyone who might be in attendance.

Be wary: if you personally subscribe to a specific faith perspective, then you might unintentionally include teachings or principles derived from your beliefs in the wedding ceremony. If the wedding couple doesn't subscribe to those same beliefs, then you might cause offense by referencing these religious principles. Remember: this day is about them, not you. You should engage in a dialogue with the couple well-in-advance of the ceremony, in order to ensure that you focus on items that are of greatest importance to them.

The Wedding Party

Knowing details about the wedding party in advance can be extremely helpful. That knowledge will allow you to cater your language to match the unique dynamics of those who will be in attendance. It would be embarrassing to refer to a woman that you assume is the groom's mother, only to find out that she is his grandmother or sister! To avoid any humiliation, make sure that you have met the wedding party and understand the relationships between everyone involved. You will find a worksheet at the back of this guide that will help you keep track of "Who's who," including members of the wedding party and the other individuals like you who are tasked with ensuring that the big day moves forward as smoothly as possible.

You might also speak with the wedding couple to see if they have preferences about the way they are addressed during the ceremony. For example, they might prefer to be called by their nickname instead of their legal name, or you might need assistance with the correct pronunciation of their names so that you say them properly during the ceremony.

Traditions

Ask the bride and groom if there are any particular traditions that should be included in the ceremony. As an example, some people like to include religious activities such as a candle lighting ceremony, a ring exchange, a handfasting, a musical performance, a scripture reading, or a communion. You can talk with the couple to determine the best place to fit those traditions into the ceremony and how they might most effectively be carried out.

These traditions might be derived from their family history/culture, or they might be based on certain religious principles. Be sure you fully understand and are respectful of the requested traditions and their significance so that you can make the bride and groom feel as comfortable as possible.

If you aren't immediately familiar with a specific tradition the couple is requesting, then you should take some time to independently study the subject. You should also speak with the bride and groom to learn more about their preferences for the way the tradition should be presented during their ceremony.

Sometimes, a wedding couple might choose non-traditional details for their ceremony. Examples could include a non-traditional song that is played during the ceremony, or even a little humor that is added in.

The Ceremony

The ceremony is one of the most significant and memorable moments in a couple's relationship, so you must ensure that you are well-prepared. You should be finished with all preparations well before the big day, as unfinished tasks will add unnecessary stress for you and for the couple.

It is best to arrive at the wedding location ahead of schedule, to allow time for gathering your thoughts, preparing yourself, answering any last-minute questions, and assisting with any last-minute preparations. You may not have an opportunity to speak with the bride or groom directly ahead of the wedding ceremony, so (again) do attempt to complete all of your preparations as fully as possible before the big day arrives.

During the ceremony, do your best to speak clearly and avoid talking too fast. As mentioned earlier in this guide, a quick visit to the location of the wedding venue can help you gauge whether or not you'll need to take any extra measures to ensure that you are heard by all of those in attendance. Additionally, make sure that you have fully rehearsed what you are going to say. If it makes you more comfortable, you might consider bringing a small card or a piece of paper containing an outline or agenda for the ceremony, as well as any other notes you might need to reference. If you use notes, please do try to do so tastefully — no bride wants to see her minister pull a crumpled-up pharmacy receipt out of her/his pocket! On our website we offer high-quality executive portfolios that can assist you in maintaining a professional appearance.

Speaking of your professional appearance, we urge you to discuss your ministerial attire with the couple in advance, so that you can dress appropriately (after all, you will be in a lot of the important photos). The Universal Life Church offers a wide selection of ministerial apparel in its online catalog; we would invite you to explore these items as you consider how to outfit yourself appropriately. Many couples will prefer that you wear a traditional black minister's shirt, while some may request more formal robes, and still others might prefer that you dress in casual attire.

In the following sections of this guide, you will see more detailed information about certain elements that may be included in the wedding ceremony. In this book's appendix, you will find a basic agenda for use during the ceremony that includes all of these. You should read through the following descriptions to gain an understanding of each of these elements. Once you have a firm grasp on them, try to carve out some time to sit down with the couple and walk them through each of the items to determine if and how they might best be included in the ceremony.

Processional

The wedding processional sets the stage for the ceremony. Its form can be adjusted according to the preferences of the wedding party.

A traditional processional usually involves the groom and best man walking through the door and standing at the front of the room, followed by the bridesmaids who are escorted by the groomsmen. Next, the maid of honor comes in, usually accompanied by the best man. Then the ring bearer comes

Processional Formation

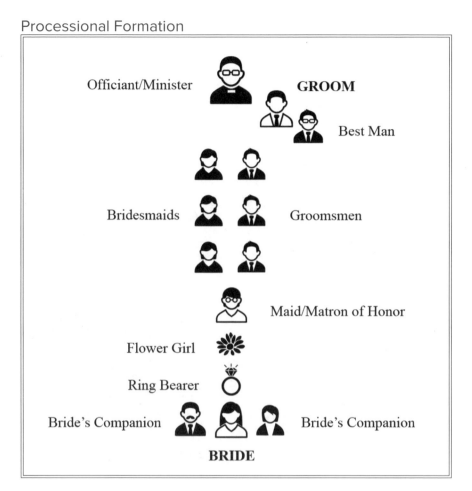

in, followed by the flower girl. The last person to enter the room is the bride, who is led down the aisle by her companion(s).

This processional may vary depending on the preferences of the couple. For example, same-sex couples sometimes choose a different processional order, or they might choose to walk down the aisle together.

During this processional, it is tradition for the wedding guests to stand as the bride enters the room. It is also common to have music playing at this time; the Bridal Chorus (the "Here Comes the Bride" song) might start playing the moment before the bride begins to walk down the aisle, signaling the guests to rise and turn toward the Bride as she makes her way down in aisle in all of her splendor.

Family Blessing

A traditional part of many wedding ceremonies is the "give away" moment when a family member escorts the bride to the groom. Often, a father, mother, or another dear relative of the bride will walk the bride down the aisle, and then participate in the family blessing. As the officiant, you can ask the family member if they are ready to give away their daughter in marriage.

Even though the "give away" is a dated tradition, it is still often included in marriage ceremonies as a formality. Historically, it is the bride's father who gives away the bride, but many couples choose to change the tradition by also including the mother. In the processional diagram presented in the appendix and on the preceding page we've labeled whoever might be giving away the bride (if this element is included) as a "Bride's Companion".

Welcome Statement

As you are starting the ceremony, you should have a welcome statement planned, and this statement can be catered to match the preferences of the couple. Your first words will set the mood for the entire ceremony, so choose them carefully. There are a number of elements that you might determine are appropriate to include in your welcoming. Commonly, welcome statements include some (or all) of the following:

✿ An acknowledgment of the guests and a sincere "Thank You" for their attendance

✿ A quick note on the significance of marriage in a relationship

✿ Any special message requested by the bride or groom

✿ An introduction of the minister, making note of her/his role as an ordained minister in assisting with the marriage vows

✿ A bit of advice or a positive message directed toward the bride and groom

Altar Formation

Above you'll find an illustration of the typical way in which the wedding party will arrange themselves at the altar following the processional. By and large, this hierarchical structure is a universal one. Of course, you and the couple can feel free to arrange yourselves in whichever way you think is most appropriate (and the venue may, in part, dictate the best organizational layout).

If the guests are still standing at this point, please ask them to be seated. You might begin by welcoming them to the ceremony, and then directing your attention to provide a warmer, more intimate greeting to the bride and groom. You can continue the welcome statement by talking about the bride and groom, or anything else that might be contextually appropriate. Here is an example of a short welcome statement that you might use:

Sample Welcome Statement

"We have gathered together today to celebrate the union of (state the names of the couple). This gift of marriage is miraculous, and this ceremony presents us with a wonderful opportunity to celebrate the love shared between these two souls."

Wedding Sermon

The sermon is the opportunity to share a message, incorporate a moment of preaching, read some scriptural passages, or recite a poem. While some people prefer that the minister deliver a more detailed sermon for their wedding, many other couples might request that the sermon be kept short and sweet.

As you are planning your sermon, make sure that you talk with the couple to determine if they want a religious or secular sermon. Traditional religious ceremonies might include a sermon that

mentions verses from religious scriptures or texts. On the other hand, a more secular sermon might include another message that isn't focused on a specific religion or set of spiritual beliefs.

Sometimes, the couple might wish to invite other people to participate in the ceremony. For example, they might ask a family member or a friend to perform a musical number, or to share some intimate words of wisdom. The sermon provides an appropriate place to incorporate those elements into the ceremony, as well as any broader messages about the special day

Remember:
The wedding day is more about the couple and
their union than it is about you!

Consecration

The consecration of the wedding ceremony is the opportunity to offer a solemn dedication for the event. This consecration might lean more religious or more secular, depending on the preferences of the wedding party. Usually, this consecration statement involves the covenant between the bride and groom, and their dedication to each other for the rest of their lives.

The consecration provides a good opportunity to share a prayer for the long-term wellbeing of the wedding couple, which can be done according to the religious beliefs of the couple.

Wedding Vows

The exchanging of wedding vows offers the couple a moment to publicly and directly express their love and devotion for one another. As the minister, you can inform the couple and the wedding guests that it is time for the couple to share their wedding vows.

The vows also provide the couple with the opportunity to share a message with their guests, if they so desire. Although vows are quite common, some wedding couples might elect to skip this element and instead share their vows in private after the ceremony. We've even heard of couples exchanging their vows via letter or handwritten note. You will need to ask the couple if they would like a moment to exchange vows, and how the vows should be implemented in case they have specific requests. The vow exchange can place couples in an unfamiliar position, and they may ask for some guidance in preparing these, so you should be prepared to gently guide them through the process.

The wedding vows will typically fall into one of three categories: traditional vows (religious), contemporary (nonreligious), or custom vows (a combination). No matter which category they fall into, the vows are essentially the message of love and commitment that the couple can promise to each other publicly. They are pure emotion expressed verbally, and can be quite touching. Quite often the minister, and even the wedding guests, will find themselves moved to tears during the vow recitals. A common thread in all vows is the promise to love each other "through thick and thin for the rest of [their] lives." They may also include promises to respect each other, take care of one another, and to work together even when the relationship faces difficulties or trials.

Traditional Vows

Traditional vows typically derive from the couple's religious background. For example, a couple getting married in the Christian tradition will likely have Christian vows. If they asked for help in writing their vows, you could offer advice if you have knowledge of Scripture, or direct them to a religious passage. You'd take the same course of action for a wedding from any other religious perspective.

Sample Traditional Vow:

I, (name), take you, (name), to be my lawfully wedded (husband/wife), my constant friend, my faithful partner and my love from this day forward. In the presence of God, our family and friends, I offer you my solemn vow to be your faithful partner in sickness and in health, in joy and in sorrow, and in life as well as in death. I promise to love you unconditionally, to honor and respect you, to laugh with you and cry with you, and to cherish you both in this life and in the next.

Contemporary Vows

Contemporary vows are typically used in non-religious weddings. Since the couple would not have a tradition to build from, they might require help from you in crafting their vows. You can offer what wisdom you have, or encourage them to research various contemporary vows, and pick the ones that speak to them.

Sample Contemporary Vow:

I take you as you are, loving who you are now and who you are yet to become. I promise to listen to you and learn from you, to support you and accept your support. I will celebrate your triumphs and mourn your losses as though they were my own. I will love you and have faith in your love for me, through all our years and all that life may bring us.

Custom Vows

Custom vows can be a combination of the two types described earlier, or completely original vows that the couple write themselves. As such, it's likely they will already have a few things in mind. If the couple does ask for your assistance, you can feel free to offer a few suggestions based on other vows you've heard, or encourage them to use the traditional vows as a base, and tweak them as necessary. They could also incorporate their favorite songs, poems, or quotes about love.

Sample Custom Vow:

(Name), I loved you from the moment I saw you in line at Starbucks and I haven't stopped loving you since. You are the most generous, and selfless person I know. You are not afraid to be yourself, and you unfailingly find joy in the most unlikely places. You are my best friend and accomplice, and I look forward to sharing cups of coffee and the rest of my life with you.

Sometimes, a couple might exchange their vows while simultaneously performing a special traditional activity. For example, they might be planning to hold hands or candles, which could make it difficult for them to hold any notes while they deliver their vows. In this case, you should make yourself available to hold up their notes so that they can see the paper while they are speaking.

As the minister, it is your duty to officiate over the ceremony and ensure it moves smoothly. That said, the minister will traditionally step back to let the couple have their moment to exchange their vows; you needn't worry about actively participating in this portion of the ceremony unless the couple specifically asks for your help.

Declaration of Intent

The declaration of intent is the moment that everyone has been waiting for: the time when the bride and groom say "I Do." Ask the wedding couple to join hands, and then address each individual. Typically, you will begin by asking one person "Do you (*Groom's name*) take (*Bride's name)* to be your lawfully wedded (*wife)*?" After the "I Do" response, you may then ask the question of the other individual. In most states, this is the only element of the ceremony that must legally occur—**you must ask this question of the bride and groom in clear terms.**

The Rings

Many couples like to exchange rings during the wedding ceremony. The ring exchange tradition is a beautiful one, and provides the couple the opportunity to display to the world their lifelong commitment and devotion to one another. The ring bearer is invited to step forward at this moment, then the bride and groom will take turns placing the ring on the finger of their spouse.

Before the ring exchange begins, you could choose to share information about the symbolism of exchanging rings. You might explain that the wedding promises are sealed with the ring exchange, and elaborate on the symbolic significance of the rings themselves. The rings not only symbolize the couple's desire to be faithful to one another, but their circular shape evokes the couple's unending commitment. These rings are important to the couple, a constant reminder of their partner's presence in the world.

The Pronouncement

Once the rings are on their fingers, you have the opportunity to officially pronounce the couple as married. The simplest way to make the pronouncement is: "I now pronounce you husband and wife." However, the language of the pronouncement can be changed in any way to match the wishes of the wedding couple.

During this pronouncement, you should make clear that you are authorized to officiate the wedding. For example, you might say something like the example presented below.

Sample Pronouncement:

"By the power vested in me, by the Universal Life Church and by the state of _____, I now pronounce you husband and wife."

The Kiss

After making the pronouncement, invite the couple to kiss as a newly married couple. This kiss is a special moment for the couple; it's a passionate celebration of their first moments as a united family.

A common way to invite the kiss is by saying: "You may now

kiss the bride." That said, you might find that in their excitement the couple may very well preempt your instructions here. This part of the ceremony is often the most treasured for the couple and their guests—stand back and let them enjoy!

The Presentation

After the kiss is complete, you can step forward to present the newly married couple to the wedding guests. This moment is the first time that they are introduced as husband and wife. Make sure you ask them how they would like to be announced; they might ask that you say something in line with the following examples.

Sample Presentation:

"I now present to you Mr. and Mrs. _____"

Here is another way that you could phrase the presentation:

Ladies and gentlemen, it is my honor to present the newly married couple: Mr. and Mrs. (groom's first name) and (bride's first name) (Last name).

Recessional

The recessional usually involves the bride and groom walking back down the aisle, followed by the rest of the wedding party in reverse of the order in which they entered.

It is a good idea to include the recessional in the rehearsal with the wedding party, because sometimes the wedding party is confused about how and when they should exit after the wedding is complete. Rehearsing this portion of the ceremony, as well as the other major portions of the ceremony, will help to clarify the movements that are expected from each of the wedding party members.

The bride and groom should have a moment to walk down

the aisle on their own before the rest of the wedding party comes down the aisle. That moment when the couple is walking down the aisle hand-in-hand provides a perfect opportunity for the wedding photographer to take some nice photos with the wedding guests on either side.

Recessional Formation

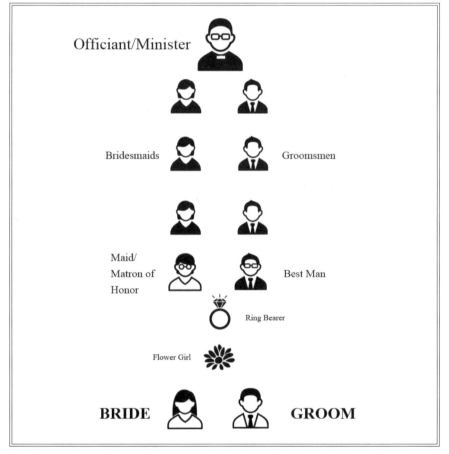

Sometimes the minister will exit immediately behind the last of the wedding party, though in many cases the couple will have some small announcements they would like the minister to share after they have exited (such as logistical information about the wedding reception). Make sure you discuss these matters with the bride and/or groom before the ceremony.

Ceremony Variations

When you are planning the ceremony with the wedding couple, it is important to consider their individual desires. Talk with them about the specific details that should be included in the ceremony, so that you can cater to their religious beliefs and personal preferences. This section will look at a few common ceremony variations that you might encounter.

Traditional

With a traditional ceremony, you will generally follow the overarching outline that was provided in the previous section of this guide. Generally, a "traditional" wedding is associated with following the customary wedding activities as dictated by the religious beliefs of the couple. It is common for different religions to have wedding ceremony traditions that are a reflection and symbol of their faith.

A traditional ceremony usually begins with a wedding

processional down the aisle including the groom, bridesmaids, groomsmen, ring bearer, flower girls, and ending with the bride and her companion(s). Make sure to welcome the wedding guests, share a positive wedding sermon, and include a consecration of the ceremony. If the Bride and Groom are of a specific religious persuasion and would like some verses read, these beginning speeches and blessings would be an ideal place to integrate those into the ceremony.

Some Common Religious Wedding Readings:

Christianity	1 Corinthians 13:4-8
Hinduism	The Saptapadi *(The 7 Steps)*
Judaism	Sheva B'rachot *(The 7 Blessings)*
Buddhism	The Buddha's sermon at Rajagaha; verses 19-22

Time must also be allotted for the declaration of intent, to give the bride and groom the chance to say their "I Dos" and share their wedding vows. In a traditional wedding ceremony, it is likely that the vows will be more structured than they would be in a more contemporary ceremony; in some religious persuasions (e.g. Catholicism) these vows may largely be pre-written for the couple and are designed to be echoed back as the Minister recites them. Most tra-

ditional wedding ceremonies will also include a ring exchange, followed by the pronunciation of the couple as "husband and wife," and the invitation for the groom to kiss his bride.

At the end of the ceremony the bride and groom will be presented by the minister as the recessional begins and they exit the wedding venue, followed by their wedding party.

Traditional wedding ceremonies may also include rituals and traditions derived from the cultural, rather than religious, heritage of the couple. These traditions can greatly vary depending on the cultural backgrounds of the families, but they all share one common theme: a symbolic expression of the commitment between the bride and groom.

Examples of traditional activities include joining the hands, exchanging rings, smashing wine glasses, jumping over brooms, drinking champagne, or participating in a chant. In Orthodox Jewish ceremonies, the bride and groom stand under a canopy known as a "chuppah," which is a symbol of the home that the couple will build together.

Contemporary

With a contemporary or modern wedding ceremony, you may include many of the same elements of the traditional wedding ceremony, but simply adjust the wording to match the desires of the bride and groom. Often, these contemporary ceremonies aren't as focused on the religious messages, and may be held in unique locations.

Contemporary ceremonies are often shorter than certain types of religious/traditional ceremonies. They can also allow couples a great deal more freedom in determining exactly how they want their ceremony carried out. Some couples will craft contemporary ceremonies designed to revolve around a certain theme (like "Star Wars"); others use the opportunity to craft a ceremony combining their two faith perspectives (i.e. Judaism and Catholicism); and still others who want a ceremony that is specifically catered to their own personal love story.

Because contemporary ceremonies are so readily customizable, we've also found that they can be held in unique locations.

Examples of contemporary wedding locations include amusement parks, beaches, golf courses, farms, or any other location that has significance for the couple.

We are often asked by ministers what readings might be appropriate for a wedding in which the Bride and Groom would prefer that traditional religious texts are not read from. There are a number of non-denominational, more spiritual readings out there to choose from, but we would recommend in particular "Union" by Robert Fulghum.

Same-Sex

Same-sex marriages are legal in most states, so you may have the opportunity to officiate at a same-sex wedding. Most of the elements of the ceremony are similar to those in any other wedding, although a few adjustments might be made to better accommodate the couple.

If you have officiated at many other weddings and this is your first time performing a same-sex wedding, then one thing that you need to be cautious about is the way you refer to the wedding couple. It can be easy to accidentally slip back into old patterns of saying "bride and groom," which certainly wouldn't be appropriate in some contexts... So be sure that you speak to the couple and discuss how they would like to be referred to during the ceremony and when they are announced.

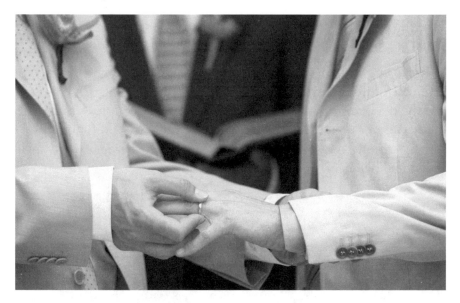

Some same-sex couples will want to have a fairly traditional wedding ceremony, while others prefer to think outside the box when it comes to planning their big day. Here are a few options that you might suggest if the couple is looking for ideas for how best to adjust the processional:

✿ Both partners can walk down the aisle together, instead of having one waiting at the front of the room while the other walks down the aisle.

✿ The partners can walk in one at a time, each being escorted by one or both of their parents.

✿ Have the seats arranged so that there are two aisles, allowing both partners to walk down their own aisle at the same time.

Because the legality of same-sex marriage varies in each state, you will need to make sure that you are planning the ceremony in accordance with local laws. As the wedding officiant, you should make the effort to understand the local laws in your area related to same-sex weddings.

Wiccan/Pagan

Wiccan and Pagan weddings tend to be very different from traditional weddings, and you will find that the ceremonies can vary widely depending on the preferences of the couples. There are many different types of Pagan worship, each with different wedding traditions. Most couples prefer a ceremony based around their individual beliefs.

Often, the ceremony will start by "casting a circle," or the couple might choose to have the circle cast a few hours before the ceremony begins. This process will likely include a time where you, as the officiant, will turn to each point on the compass in order to honor the four elements: air, fire, water, and earth.

Sometime the circle might contain an altar, and traditional items might be placed on that altar. These traditional items might include things such as a trowel, knife, and a cup. There may also be things to represent each of the four elements, such as water, a feather symbolizing air, a candle for the fire, and salt for the earth.

Pagans tend to be egalitarian, which means that it is unlikely the bride will be given away by her father. Some families have traditional activities to honor the living family members as well as the ancestors who have passed on. It is also common for the couple to approach the circle and enter it from the East coordinate, an action which symbolizes the rise/growth of their relationship.

It is common in the 21st century that a Wiccan or Pagan wedding will include elements that could also be found in a more "traditional" wedding ceremony. For example, the couple might want some time included in the ceremony to share their vows with their significant other and the assembled circle, or to exchange rings with one another. Speak to the couple about what they'd like included.

Handfasting

Handfasting is often included in Pagan or Wiccan weddings, but is also a common element in many modern-day Celtic and Irish weddings. It features the couple joining their hands together as the minister wraps a ribbon or cord around the joined hands.

Even though the tradition of handfasting is commonly associated with a particular set of beliefs, this beautiful ritual may be included in any other type of wedding ceremony. Alternately, the handfasting ritual can be expanded to form the entirety of the ceremony, if the couple chooses to forgo a more 'traditional' wedding. You can find a fuller guide to performing handfastings on our site.

Handfasting is a traditional way of showing their commitment for each other, and it is common for the wedding couple to share their vows while their hands are tied together.

Originally, handfasting was the representation of a trial marriage, where the couple would stay together for a year before re-assessing their commitment and love to determine if they wanted to stay together. Even though the origins of handfasting were related to a trial marriage, today handfasting is usually a symbol of life-long commitment, and the couple will often consider the marriage to be permanent.

If you are officiating at a wedding ceremony that includes

handfasting, you should begin by asking the couple to join their hands together. Usually, the bride and groom will cross their arms and clasp both of their partner's hands. The joining hands and arms creates the "infinity" symbol, signifying the eternal love that they share.

Once the hands are joined, you will use a ribbon or cord to wrap around their hands and join them together. Some couples might choose to share their vows while their hands are tied together. If that is the case, you (the officiant) might need to assist by holding their notes so that each person can deliver their vows accurately.

After you have pronounced the couple as married, and the groom has the opportunity to kiss the bride, then a few more traditional activities may be included. For example, they might feed something to one other, or bury the handfasting cord or locks of their hair.

Sometimes, the guests will arrange themselves in a circle around the bride and groom (a particularly popular choice at outdoor weddings where such an arrangement is especially convenient). If the guests are in a circle, it is common for the couple to walk around the circle in order to greet their family and friends after. The circle will be de-consecrated once the ceremony is complete.

Renewal of Vows

A renewal of vows isn't a "legal" ceremony because the "bride" and "groom" are already married. A vow renewal allows the wedding couple to recommit and publicly share their love and devotion. This vow renewal is often held around the marriage anniversary.

Sometimes wedding couples plan to renew their vows during certain notable anniversaries, such as their five-year, ten-year, twenty-year, or fifty-year anniversary. Other times, a vow renewal may be the opportunity for a couple to recommit and bond together again after going through a rough patch in their relationship. There isn't a right or wrong time for a couple to renew their vows, it's entirely up to them!

As the officiant, you can cater the script to match the desires of the couple. You might retain some of the same phrasing that was used in their traditional wedding ceremony, but change a few words as required.

For example, you might say, "Do you reaffirm your love, and promise to cherish and honor him/her in health and in sickness... Etc." Then, each partner will have the opportunity to say, "I Do."

One special moment of a vow renewal is when the couple shares their vows. Since the couple has spent time together in marriage, they often have a special, unique message to share with their spouse. This message might be especially tailored if the couple has recently undergone a particularly challenging period of time.

Vow renewal ceremonies will often include any children the couple have. Younger children can easily be integrated in the same flower girl/ring bearer roles that they might play in an ordinary wedding. Adult children can be incorporated as well: in one of the more emotionally touching vow renewal ceremonies I've personally attended, the couple's children were all ordained ministers of the Universal Life church and acted together as co-officiants of their parents' ceremony.

Simple

Some couples don't want to go through the stress of planning a big wedding and would prefer to avoid getting caught up in all the details. A simple wedding offers these people the opportunity to share

their commitment to each other and legally wed without organizing a massive party.

A simple ceremony might be boiled down only to include the essentials: as noted earlier, often just the Declaration of Intent with the witnesses present. Afterwards, the paperwork must still be signed and submitted. The rest of the elements of the wedding are spiritual and emotional additions that can make the ceremony a nicer occasion and a memorable event for all in attendance, but are not necessarily legally required.

Each bride has her own definition of "simple." A simple ceremony for one bride might involve a ceremony in a beautiful venue that doesn't require much adornment with a dozen or so guests, while a simple ceremony for another bride might take place in the couple's home and only include the bride, the groom and whatever witnesses are legally mandated.

If you are asked to officiate a simple wedding, then you should talk with the wedding couple to understand how long they would like the ceremony to last. As the officiant, it is your job to make sure that you don't ramble on too long. You might just deliver a short, positive message, let the couple exchange their vows (if they so-desire), then invite them to share their "I Dos" and a kiss as husband and wife.

Just because a ceremony is "simple" or quick doesn't mean that it isn't a deeply meaningful one for the couple... keep this in mind as you speak to the couple about their preferences.

After the Ceremony

O nce the wedding ceremony is complete, it is easy to assume that your job is done. But, there are a few additional details to keep in mind. The following chapter will cover all of the things you need to accomplish after the "I Dos" are exchanged.

Filling Out the Marriage License

The first of your two primary legal responsibilities as the wedding officiant is to ensure the marriage license is properly filled out. You should fully review and confirm that you understand the protocol for completing a marriage license in your area, particularly if you intend to officiate more than one ceremony.

Fortunately, marriage licenses are typically fairly straightforward documents. If you have any questions or concerns about its proper completion as you are filling it out, we would urge you to seek clarification from the issuing office.

We often get calls from our ministers seeking clarification about certain terms that appear in the marriage license. Below, you'll find definitions for some of the words and phrases you will likely encounter as you navigate the legal half of marriage.

Waiting Period:
The period of time between when a couple applies for a marriage license and when it will be issued by the local marriage authority. Note that in some areas there may also be a waiting period between when the marriage license is issued and when the ceremony may legally take place.

Expiration:
Marriage licenses do expire! This number indicates the amount of time after the marriage license is issued during which the wedding ceremony can be conducted.

Return:
The amount of time between when the license has been signed and when it must be returned (in many areas it just needs to be returned before expiry, though some counties have more stringent guidelines).

The document will likely need to be signed both by you (as the officiant) and by the couple after the ceremony is complete. Some areas may require that additional witnesses sign the marriage license as well. Keep in mind that as an ordained member of the Universal Life Church your official legal title is "Minister" as you are filling out this document. Also note that, as an ordained minister, any wedding ceremony that you officiate will be, in the eyes of the law, "Religious" as opposed to "Civil." In your capacity as a wedding officiant you are acting as both the legal and ecclesiastical representative of the "Universal Life Church", a non-denominational religious organization.

Please exercise caution as you are completing the license: if it is not filled out properly, it might result in the nullification of the marriage. In some areas, filling out the marriage license incorrectly could even result in your ability to officiate weddings being revoked by the local authorities.

Filing the Marriage License with the Clerk

Your other primary legal responsibility as the wedding officiant is to submit the marriage license to the local marriage authority. This is either the county, city, or state marriage office depending on the location where the wedding was performed. If this is not done correctly, the couple may encounter problems with the legality of their marriage.

Keep in mind that many states have a specific time frame in which the marriage license paperwork must be received (for example, you might be required to return the completed and signed license to the issuing office within 10 days of the ceremony), so it is important that the paperwork be submitted as soon as possible after the wedding. It is typical in most counties that at least one member of the couple-to-be-wed will be required to visit the local marriage authority to apply for and receive an unsigned copy of their marriage license (though in many jurisdictions, both members of the couple must present themselves). Either the couple or the officiant can return the properly signed license back to the local marriage authority, though traditionally this responsibility falls on the minister.

The issuing office should deliver specific instructions about the proper return of the marriage license to the couple when it is issued, those instructions supersede any general advice given here.

If you are entrusted with the delivery of the marriage license, be extremely careful with it. Aside from its symbolic value, the document has enormous legal weight. Again, the best strategy is to submit this license as soon as it has been properly filled out; the window of time in which it must be returned after the ceremony can be as short as a handful of days.

Traditionally, the wedding officiant will also sign a commemorative marriage certificate for the couple. This document is not the same as a marriage license, and it is important that you understand the difference between the two. A *marriage license* is a document maintained by the state which officially records the names of the parties getting married, the date of their ceremony, their signatures, and the signatures of the officiant and the ceremony's witnesses. On the other hand, a *marriage certificate* is a decorative document marking the details of the marriage that the couple can keep in their personal files or even frame and display in their home or among their wedding photos. A marriage certificate is a lovely keepsake for a minister to gift a couple upon completion of the ceremony, one that they will treasure forever.

If you plan to perform more than one marriage ceremony (and we do find that many of our ministers enjoy officiating so much that they will go on to perform more ceremonies!) it is a good practice to maintain a comprehensive file of the weddings that you have officiated. We would recommend that, if possible, you make at least two photocopies of the signed marriage license before it is submitted to the local marriage authority—one for you and one for the couple. Having a copy on-hand can be an invaluable resource in case the original is lost, stolen, damaged, or if you are asked to testify regarding the validity of the marriage.

Congratulations! If you've made it this far in the book, you are now a bona fide expert on performing wedding ceremonies. Whether this is your first ceremony or your hundredth ceremony, we're sure that, armed with the knowledge from this guide, you will do magnificently. As an ordained minister and wedding officiant, you play an important role in human society, and we're happy to provide you with all of the tools you need to reach your full potential.

If you are left with any questions or concerns, you are invited to contact the friendly support staff of the Universal Life Church Ministries by emailing help@themonastery.org.

Appendix

Officiating a wedding is an incredibly fulfilling experience, but it is not always an easy undertaking (and it can be especially challenging if it is your first time). Even seasoned officiants need to remember names, dates, numbers, and various procedural information; all of these details can sometimes be overwhelming.

To assist you, we've compiled a number of worksheets to help organize all of this information and aid in planning a complete and personalized wedding ceremony. You will find, among other things, checklists to ensure that you've completed everything you need to complete, lists of important questions to ask the couple, and a ceremony agenda to aid you while you are up at the altar.

We encourage you to make use of these resources, so that you remain organized and the ceremony flows smoothly. As plans come together, keep a record of them here so that no detail is overlooked. Take notes, make copies, and don't worry! With this guide in hand, you are well on your way to presiding over a special and memorable wedding ceremony.

Pre-Ceremony Checklist

☐ Get ordained online at *www.themonastery.org/ordination*.

☐ Contact the local county clerk to determine what paper-work you'll need to officiate a legally valid marriage.

☐ Communicate with the couple about your responsibilities as officiant and your fee. Secure a deposit and save the date.

☐ Order necessary documents (credentials, letter of good standing, marriage certificates, etc.) and submit these to clerk before the wedding.

☐ Speak with the couple about their ceremony. There are a number of questions that should be asked; we've provided a few on the following page to get you started.

☐ Make sure that the couple has acquired the marriage license and has it in-hand at the time of the ceremony.

☐ Prepare your script and understand your place in the itinerary. If necessary, you might find it helpful to have some notes prepared for reference.

☐ Coordinate your attire with the couple. It's their special day, you should dress yourself according to their wishes.

☐ During the rehearsal ceremony, finalize the script and ensure that everyone involved in the ceremony understands the itinerary and their individual role.

☐ Arrive at the wedding location well ahead of schedule, making yourself available to answer any last minute questions.

☐ Bring a pen so you can sign and submit the marriage license!

Questions for the Couple

- ✿ Do you have a location in mind or reserved? Will I (the minister) need a microphone to be heard by the guests?

- ✿ Do you plan on holding a wedding rehearsal?

- ✿ Is there a wedding planner/manager who will be running the rehearsal? Or would you prefer that I direct it?

- ✿ Where will you be acquiring and filing the marriage license?

- ✿ Is there any faith-specific language you'd like included in the ceremony?

- ✿ Are there any special traditions (candle-lighting, handfasting, etc.) you'd like included in the ceremony?

- ✿ Which names would you prefer to go by during the ceremony (some couples prefer not to use their nicknames)? How would you like to be announced at the end?

- ✿ How long would you like the ceremony to be?

- ✿ Would you mind if I used a script during the ceremony?

- ✿ Will you be writing/reading your own vows?

- ✿ What would you like me to wear?

- ✿ Would you like to review my entire script/wedding sermon?

- ✿ How long would you like your ceremony to last?

- ✿ Are there any special instructions (e.g. directions to the reception) that you'd like me to deliver after you've exited the venue as husband and wife?

Dates, Times, Names & Faces

The Wedding Party

Bride:_____ Groom: _____

Maid of Honor: _____ Best Man: _____

Bridesmaids: Groomsmen:

_____ _____

_____ _____

_____ _____

_____ _____

_____ _____

Flower Girl:_____ Ring Bearer:_____

Key Contacts

Officiant: _____ Phone:_____

Planner:_____ Phone:_____

Photo: _____ Phone:_____
Video: _____ Phone:_____
Sound:_____ Phone:_____
Florist:_____ Phone:_____

Dates & Times

The Rehearsal   *The Ceremony*

Date: _____ Date: _____

Time:_____ Time:_____

Location:_____ Location:_____

Contact:_____ Contact:_____

Ceremony Agenda

Ceremony begins at: _____ AM/PM

Party and Key People arrive by: _____ AM/PM

Processional

Music, Entry of Bridal Party: _____
Music, Entry of Bride: _____
Family Blessing

Wedding Ceremony Begins

Welcome Statement
Wedding Sermon
Readings
Consecration
Declaration of Intent
Wedding Vows
Ring Explanation
Ring Exchange
Alternative Tradition (*optional*)
The Pronouncement
The Kiss
The Presentation

Recessional

Music, Exit: _____

Additional Announcements:

Processional Formation

The processional marks the start of the ceremony, and is typically kick-started by the playing of the Bridal Chorus. While in some cases the groom begins the ceremony already standing at the altar, it is becoming more commonplace that he will start a "pre-processional" by walking the aisle with his mother. Other close family members may follow. Guests traditionally stand as the Bride enters.

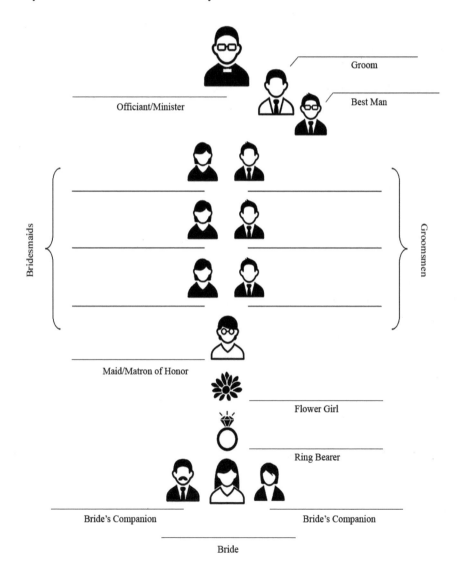

Recessional Formation

The recessional begins the moment the officiant presents the couple to the wedding's guests. The Minister may either follow the wedding party out, or remain to deliver any announcements that the Bride and Groom would like shared with their guests before these people exit. Make sure you understand what the couple expects. Guests may or may not stand and applaud as the couple exits.

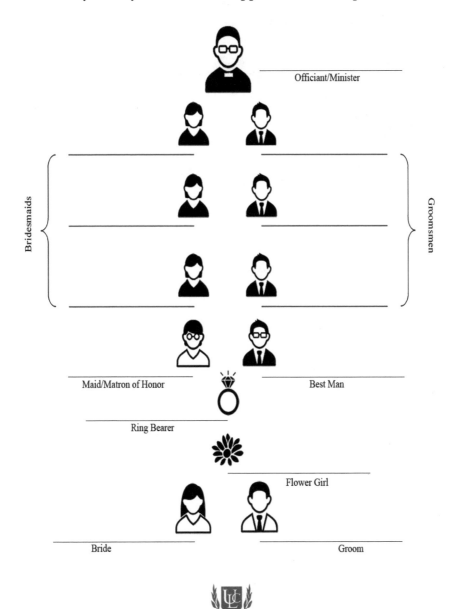

Officiant/Minister

Bridesmaids

Groomsmen

Maid/Matron of Honor

Best Man

Ring Bearer

Flower Girl

Bride

Groom

Altar Formation

The wedding party will spend the majority of their time at the altar during the ceremony. We've found that many couples prefer to organize themselves in the traditional hierarchical layout presented below, but feel free to get creative!

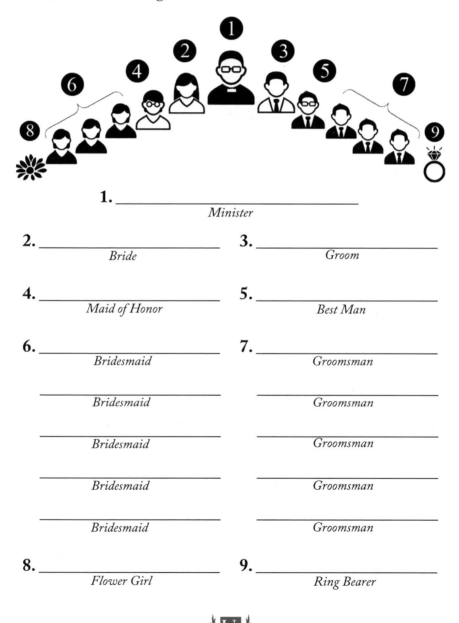

1. _____
Minister

2. _____ **3.** _____
Bride   *Groom*

4. _____ **5.** _____
Maid of Honor   *Best Man*

6. _____ **7.** _____
Bridesmaid   *Groomsman*

_____ _____
Bridesmaid   *Groomsman*

_____ _____
Bridesmaid   *Groomsman*

_____ _____
Bridesmaid   *Groomsman*

_____ _____
Bridesmaid   *Groomsman*

8. _____ **9.** _____
Flower Girl   *Ring Bearer*

Making it Meaningful

If you don't know the couple you are marrying well, you might find it helpful to ask them a couple of questions to make the ceremony all the more special. The information gained can help you in preparing your greeting-sermon and/or can be used to aid the couple in preparing their vows. Below you'll find a few to get you started.

How did you meet?

_____

_____

_____

What initially drew you together?

_____

_____

_____

What was your proposal like?

_____

_____

_____

What do you like most about "A"?

_____

_____

_____

What do you like most about "B"?

_____

_____

_____

What's the best adventure you've had together?

_____

_____

_____

Notes

_____
_____
_____
_____
_____
_____
_____
_____
_____
_____
_____
_____
_____
_____
_____
_____
_____
_____
_____
_____
_____
_____
_____
_____
_____
_____
_____
_____
_____
_____
_____
_____
_____

Notes

_____
_____
_____
_____
_____
_____
_____
_____
_____
_____
_____
_____
_____
_____
_____
_____
_____
_____
_____
_____
_____
_____
_____
_____
_____
_____
_____
_____
_____
_____
_____
_____

Notes

Notes

Notes

Notes

Notes

Notes

About the Author

    Brother G. Martin Freeman founded and leads the largest and most active branch of the Universal Life Church. His nonprofit church has ordained millions of ministers around the world. Many of these ministers get ordained online to perform weddings, baptisms, funerals, and/or to start their own churches. He has personally officiated hundreds of weddings and, in the process, become something of an expert. He hopes the knowledge he's accumulated and included in this guide will aid you in making some lucky couple's special day all the more special.

    Brother G. Martin Freeman's work in transforming the institution of the Universal Life Church has ushered a new kind of religion into the 21st century – a religion unburdened by lofty hierarchal authority. Every day he strives to do good in his universe, and he's pleased that the Universal Life Church has empowered millions of others across the planet to do the same.

For More Info...

We're happy that our flagship website has become the Internet's number one source for ordination, church supplies, information about other religions, and information related to the performance of weddings and other ceremonies. Below you'll find direct linking information to a few sections of the site that you might find particularly useful.

Become a minister so that you can legally perform a wedding:
http://www.themonastery.org/ordination

Info about state marriage laws. You can look up your location:
http://www.themonastery.org/wedding-laws/

Our wedding training section:
http://www.themonastery.org/wedding-training/

Wedding supplies that you might need, such as marriage certificates, ordination credentials, and full wedding packages:
http://www.themonastery.org/catalog/

Connect with other ministers in our Ministerial social network:
http://ministers.themonastery.org/

Frequently asked questions about ordination and officiating:
http://www.themonastery.org/catalog/faq.php

Need more information? Contact our support staff anytime by emailing **help@themonastery.org** or by dialing **(206) 285-1086** during regular business hours (Pacific Time).

"The Internet's largest church and best source of ministerial supplies."

While the Universal Life Church is most renowned for its provision of online of ordinations and its scores of proud and powerful ministers, it's also famous for its enormous collection of religious and spiritual books and supplies.

In the Minister's Supply catalog you'll find a number of books pertaining to various religious perspectives (including Christianity, Atheism, Wicca, and more) as well as books detailing how various ceremonies can best be conducted.

You'll also find a number of other special ULC goods, like apparel and accessories to help you proudly display your ministerial status!